ABLUTION
BOOK FOR MUSLIM KIDS

28 pages 8 x 10 in

* * * * *

This book belongs to:

....

....

....

بإسم الله الرحمان الرحيم

« bismi llahi rra7maani rra7iimi »

<u>In the name of Allah, Most Gracious,
Most Merciful.</u>

If you want to pray, you should keep yourself in state of clean and pure. And so as to be so, you have to perform ablution.
"Prayer without ablution is invalid »

Indeed, ablution « ALWUDU » is an islamic procedure for cleansing the whole body or parts of it. The ablution is normally done in preparation for formal daily five obligatory prayers or before handling and reading the Quran.

There are three types of ablution:

1/ Full ablution: washing the whole body using water after sexual intercourse, childbirth or menstruation.

2/ Partial ablution: washing parts of the body using water. This type of ablution is an acte for purifying some activities such as urination, defecation, flatulence, deep sleep, light bleeding. This ablution is perfomed everyday.

3/ Dry ablution: « Attayamoume »: replacing water with stone or sand when there is no water.

In this book, we will present for you how you can perfom islamic partial ablution step by step so as to practice your daily prayers correctly.

So, when someone determines to cleanse oneself for prayer, for the sake of Allah. Then, one begins with :

بإسم الله الرحمان الرحيم
« bismillahi rra7maani rra7iime »
In the name of Allah, Most Gracious,
Most Merciful.

And with water, one
then begins to wash some parts of one's body as follows:

1/ Wash the hands three times, making sure that the water reaches between the fingers and all over the hands up to the wrist

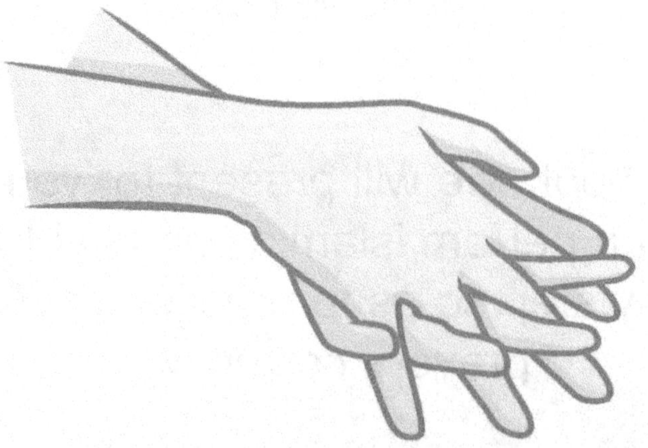

2/ Wash the mouth three times, bringing a handful of water to the mouth and rinsing thoroughly

3/ Wash the nose three times, using the right hand to bring water up to the nose, sniffing the water, and using the left hand to expel it.

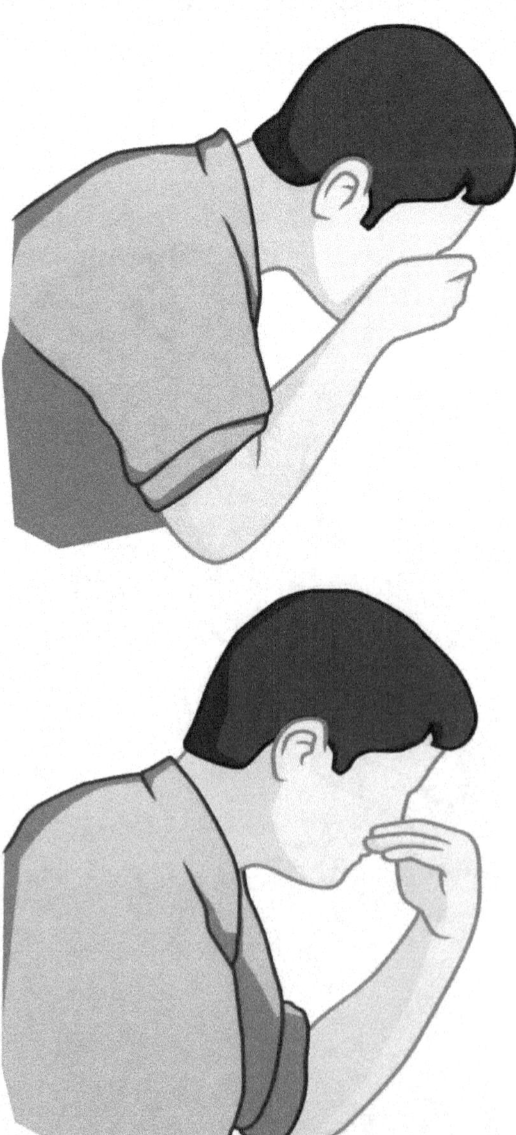

4/ Wash the face three times, from the forehead to the chin and from ear to ear.

5/ Wash the arms three times, up to the elbows, starting with the right arm.

First, the right arm.

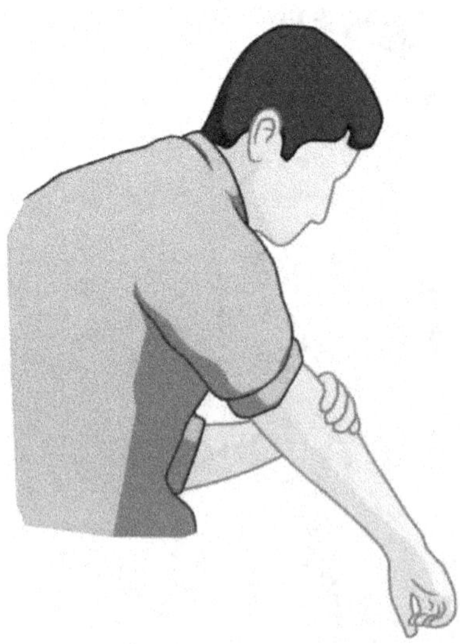 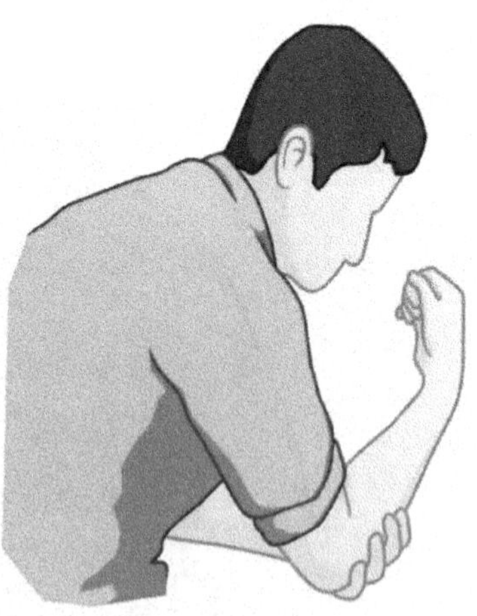

Then, the left arm.

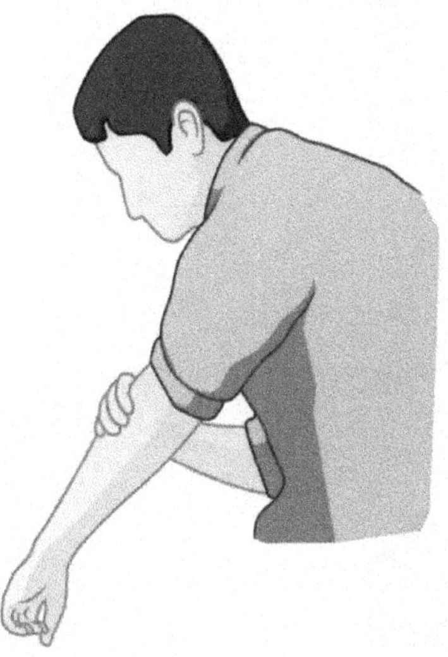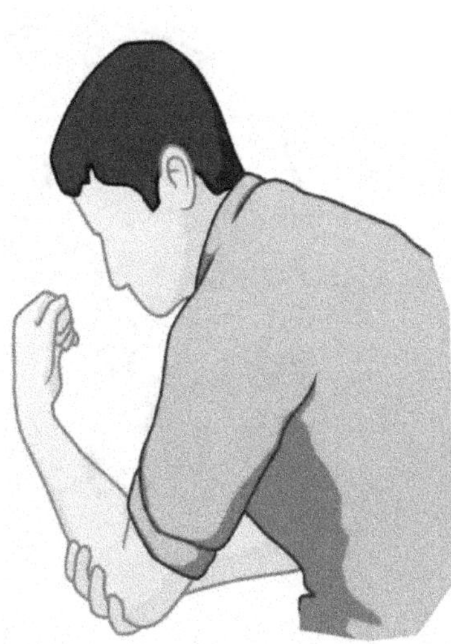

6/ Wash the head one time, using wet Hands to wipe over the head from front to back and front again.

7/ Wash the ears one time, using wet fingers to wipe the inside and outside of the ears.

8/ Wash the feet three times, up to
the ankles, starting with the right.

So, first the right foot.

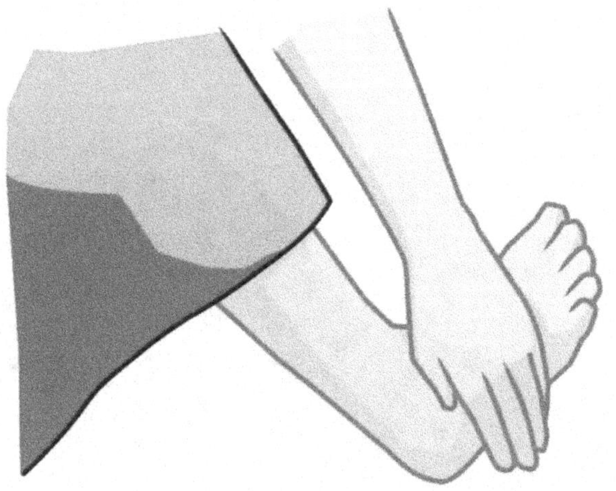

Then, wash the left foot.

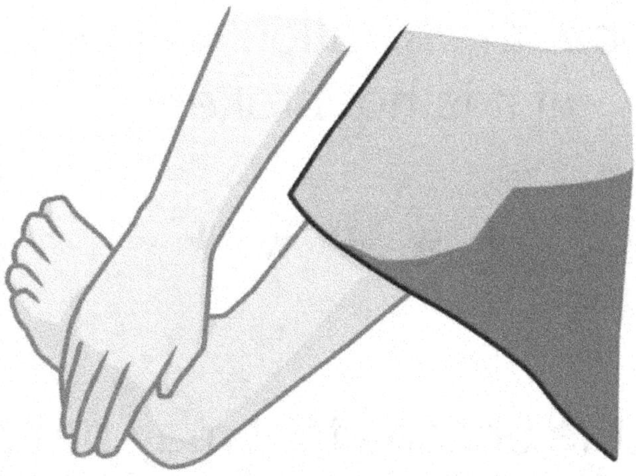

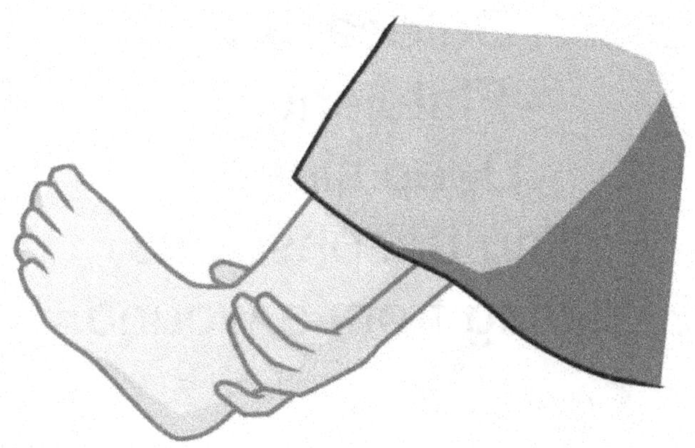

It's very important to mention that
before each everyday prayer,
the muslim person does not need
to repeat the ablution « al wudu »
if it is not broken.

* * * * *

And the actions that may break
the ablude include:
- Urination,
- Defecation,
- Flatulence,
- Deep sleep,
Falling unconscious,
Bleeding from a wound.

Now, we will present for you some DUAs
from the Quran. Indeed, these Duas
are quranic verses. And you can
use them during your prayers or after
performing them.You can also use them
whenever you want.

So, let's start

بإسم الله الرحمان الرحيم
« bismi llahi rra7maani rra7iime »
In the name of Allah, Most Gracious,
Most Merciful.

بِسْمِ اللهِ الرَّحْمَنِ الرَّحِيمِ

« bismillahi rrahmani rrahime »
In the Name of Allâh, the Most Beneficent, the Most Merciful.

سورة الحشر : Surah *Al-Hashr (Ayaa 10)*

" رَبَّنَا اغْفِرْ لَنَا وَلِإِخْوَانِنَا الَّذِينَ سَبَقُونَا بِالْإِيمَانِ وَلَا تَجْعَلْ فِي قُلُوبِنَا غِلًّا لِلَّذِينَ آمَنُوا رَبَّنَا إِنَّكَ رَءُوفٌ رَحِيمٌ. "

« rabbanaa ghfire lanaa wa li ikhwaaninaa lladiina saba9ounaa bil iimaani, wa laa taj3ale fii 9ouloubinaa ghillane lilladiina aamanou, rabbanaa innaka ra2oufoune ra7iimoune. »

« Our Lord. Forgive us, and our brethren who came before us into the Faith, and leave not, in our hearts, rancour against those who have believed. Our Lord! Thou art indeed Full of Kindness, Most Merciful. »

سورة نوح : Surah Nooh (Ayaa 28)

رَبِّ اغْفِرْ لِي وَلِوَالِدَيَّ وَلِمَنْ دَخَلَ بَيْتِيَ مُؤْمِنًا وَلِلْمُؤْمِنِينَ وَالْمُؤْمِنَاتِ وَلَا تَزِدِ الظَّالِمِينَ إِلَّا تَبَارًا

« rabbi ghfire lii wa li waalidayya wa limane dakhala bayetii mou2minane , wa lilmou2miniina wa lmou2minaati, wa laa tazidi ddalimiina illaa tabarane. »

« My Lord. Forgive me, and my parents, and him who enters my home as a believer, and all the believing men and women. And to the Zâlimûn (polytheists, wrong-doers, and disbelievers) grant You no increase but destruction. »

سورة الممتحنة : Surah AL Mumtahina

رَبَّنَا عَلَيْكَ تَوَكَّلْنَا وَإِلَيْكَ أَنَبْنَا وَإِلَيْكَ الْمَصِيرُ (4)

« rabbanaa 3alayeka tawakkalnaa wa ilayeka
anabnaa wa ilayeka lmasiirou »

« Our Lord. in Thee do we trust, and to Thee
do we turn in repentance: to Thee is Final
Goal. »

Surah AL Mumtahina : سورة الممتحنة

رَبَّنَا لَا تَجْعَلْنَا فِتْنَةً لِلَّذِينَ كَفَرُوا وَاغْفِرْ لَنَا رَبَّنَا إِنَّكَ أَنْتَ الْعَزِيزُ الْحَكِيمُ (5)

« rabbanaa laa taj3alnaa fitnatane lilladiina kafarou wa ghfire lanaa, rabbanaa innaka aneta l3azizou l7akimou. »

"Our Lord. Make us not a trial for the Unbelievers, but forgive us, our Lord. for Thou art the Exalted in Might, the Wise."

سورة الدخان : **Sura Ad-Dukhaan (Ayaa 12)**

رَبَّنَا اكْشِفْ عَنَّا الْعَذَابَ إِنَّا مُؤْمِنُونَ

« rabbanaa kshif 3annaa l3adaaba innaa mou2minouna. »

"Our Lord. Remove the torment from us, really we shall become believers."

سورة يونس: Surah Surah Yunus

فَقَالُوا عَلَى اللَّهِ تَوَكَّلْنَا رَبَّنَا لَا تَجْعَلْنَا فِتْنَةً لِلْقَوْمِ الظَّالِمِينَ (85)

« fa9aalou 3alaa llahi tawakkalnaa, rabbanaa laa taj3alnaa fitnatane lil9awemi ddalimiina »

« They said: In Allâh we put our trust. Our Lord. Make us not a trial for the folk who are Zâlimûn (polytheists and wrong-doers).»

Surah Surah Yunus :سورة يونس

وَنَجِّنَا بِرَحْمَتِكَ مِنَ الْقَوْمِ الْكَافِرِينَ (86)

« wa najjinaa bi ra7matika mina l9awemi lkaafiriina. »

« And save us by Your Mercy from the disbelieving folk. »

Surah At-Tawba : سورة التوبة

حَسْبُنَا اللَّهُ سَيُؤْتِينَا اللَّهُ مِنْ فَضْلِهِ وَرَسُولُهُ إِنَّا إِلَى اللَّهِ رَاغِبُون
(59)

« 7asbouna llahou sayou2tiinaa llahou mine fadlihi wa rasoulouhou, innaa ilaa llahi raaghibouna »

« Allâh is Sufficient for us. Allâh will give us of His Bounty, and so will His Messenger. We implore Allâh. »

<h1 style="text-align:center">Surah At-Tawba : سورة التوبة</h1>

حَسْبِيَ اللَّهُ لَا إِلَهَ إِلَّا هُوَ عَلَيْهِ تَوَكَّلْتُ وَهُوَ رَبُّ الْعَرْشِ الْعَظِيمِ (129)

« 7asbiya llahou, laa ilaaha illa houwa, 3alayehi tawakkaltou, wa houwa rabbou l3arshi l3adiimi.»

"Allâh is sufficient for me. Lâ ilâha illa Huwa (none has the right to be worshipped but He) in Him I put my trust and He is the Lord of the Mighty Throne. »

سورة المائدة : Suah AL Ma'idah (Ayaa 83)

رَبَّنَا آمَنَّا فَاكْتُبْنَا مَعَ الشَّاهِدِينَ

« rabbanaa aamannaa, faketoubenaa ma3a shaahidiina »

« Our Lord. We believe; so write us down among the witnesses. »

Surah Al-Qasas سورة القصص:

قَالَ رَبِّ إِنِّي ظَلَمْتُ نَفْسِي فَٱغْفِرْ لِي فَغَفَرَ لَهُۥٓ إِنَّهُۥ هُوَ ٱلْغَفُورُ ٱلرَّحِيمُ (16)

« 9aala rabbi innii dalamtou nafsii faghfire lii, faghafara lahou innahou houwa lghafourou rra7iimou. »

« He said: My Lord. Verily, I have wronged myself, so forgive me. Then He forgave him. Verily, He is the Oft-Forgiving, the Most Merciful. »

سورة القصص: Surah Al-Qasas

رَبِّ نَجِّنِي مِنَ الْقَوْمِ الظَّالِمِينَ (21)

« rabbi najjinii mina l9awemi ddalimiina. »

« My Lord! Save me from the people who are wrong-doers (Zâlimûn) »

سورة القصص :Surah Al-Qasas

رَبِّ إِنِّي لِمَا أَنْزَلْتَ إِلَيَّ مِنْ خَيْرٍ فَقِيرٌ (24)

« rabbi innii limaa anezalta ilayya mine khayerine fa9iirou. »

« My Lord. truly, I am in need of whatever good that You bestow on me. »